FEEDING *the* MASSES

MEAL PLANNING for Events, Large Groups, Ward Parties, **AND MORE**

PRAISE FOR *FEEDING THE MASSES*

"*I recommend this book* to anyone who is cooking for large groups. It takes all the stress out of trying to figure out amounts and what to cook. Great recipes too!"

—*Liz Edmunds,* BYUtv's The Food Nanny

"*This book is genius;* a hostess's dream. . . . Every friend, neighbor, and member of a family of any size should have this in their home . . . and use it."

—*Jordan Page,* the Fun, Cheap, or Free Queen (www.funcheaporfree.com)

"*It's a party planner tool* with menu suggestions, recipe ideas, and everything you need to know to feed the people you love food that they'll love!"

—*Rebecca Cressman,* host of *Living Essentials* on BYUtv and radio host on FM 100.3

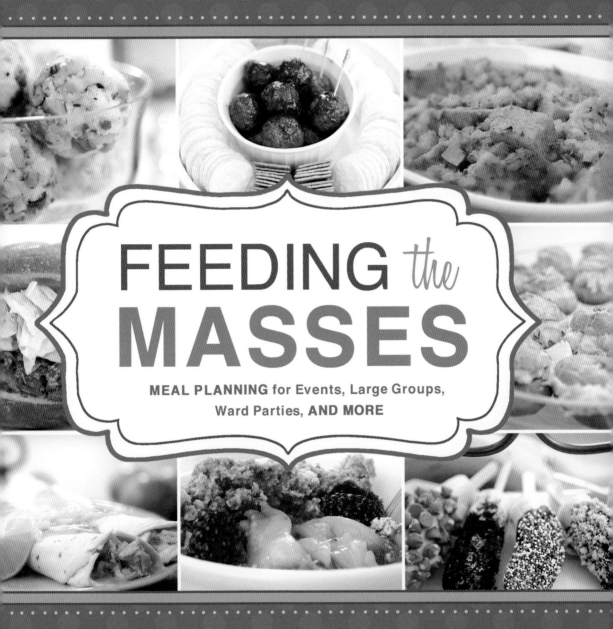

FEEDING *the* MASSES

MEAL PLANNING for Events, Large Groups,
Ward Parties, **AND MORE**

SYDNEY CLINE

Front Table Books | Springville, Utah

DEDICATION

This book is dedicated with gratitude to my mother, who was a great cook and taught me well. To my sister Leslie, who inspired me to stretch myself in every way. I express deep appreciation for my selfless son Travis, who did most of the fine photography for the book. And to my sweet daughter, Jillian, who encouraged me above all others to pursue the publication of this book. Most importantly, I dedicate this book with love and appreciation for my husband for being my first assistant at every event and quietly supporting everyone in the background. There are many, many people I have served with, learned from, and loved as I have acquired this knowledge and I applaud them for their dedication to serve others. I will hold all of them deeply in heart, always.

Text © 2012 Sydney Cline
Photographs © 2012 Travis Cline, except on pp. v, 11, 21, 27, 47, 53, 63, 72, 83, and 101
All rights reserved.

No part of this book may be reproduced in any form whatsoever, whether by graphic, visual, electronic, film, microfilm, tape recording, or any other means, without prior written permission of the publisher, except in the case of brief passages embodied in critical reviews and articles.

ISBN: 978-1-4621-1071-1

Published by Front Table Books, an imprint of Cedar Fort, Inc., 2373 W. 700 S., Springville, UT 84663
Distributed by Cedar Fort, Inc., www.cedarfort.com

LIBRARY OF CONGRESS CATALOGING-IN-PUBLICATION DATA

Cline, Sydney (Sydney L.), 1952- , author.
 Feeding the masses / Sydney Cline.
     pages cm.
 Summary: A resource guide for feeding large groups of people.
 ISBN 978-1-4621-1071-1
 1. Quantity cooking. 2. Entertaining. I. Title.
 TX820.C56 2012
 642'.4--dc23
                         2012008008

Cover and page design by Erica Dixon
Cover design © 2012 by Lyle Mortimer
Edited by Whitney A. Lindsley and Michelle Stoll

Printed in China

10 9 8 7 6 5 4 3 2 1

Printed on acid-free paper

TABLE OF CONTENTS

Introduction

Themes

Large Groups

Serving Adults

Adult Brunch Assortment

Serving Teens and Kids

Scouts and Camping

Refreshments

Potluck Events

INTRODUCTION

"We serve the people we love . . .

Welcome to your latest opportunity to serve others: by planning, purchasing, preparing, serving, or teaching others about food.

These many new responsibilities can be overwhelming, but there is hope and assistance contained in this book, which will help anyone willing to share the joy of food with others.

Whether you find yourself responsible for feeding the masses, teaching others to cook, or coordinating events, this collection of ideas, themes, organizational tools, suggestions, and recipes is a helpful resource to guide you along your way.

Be sure to record your own notes as you utilize this content, so you will continue to elaborate on what I have included. Your personal touches, of course, are unique and valuable, so trust your instincts and feel free to make changes to any of my ideas. Record the inspired thoughts you receive because you will want to use them again in the future.

My main purpose is to share my thoughts to help others get organized and hopefully simplify their path to a fun and successful event. You can create a wonderful food experience by using the help, tips, and recipes contained in this book, as well as those in other cookbooks, family files, the Internet, and your personal recipe file.

Serving in a capacity in which food is "on the menu" requires a combination of easygoing fun, delectable taste, nutritional value, and educational opportunities. By no means do need to be these experiences be so simple that they are boring, but they must not be so elaborate that the rest of your life needs to come to a

and we *love* the people we serve."

standstill until the event is over. A hot dog meal isn't always the most economical or healthy, but through creativity, it can be the foundation of a fun, new hot dog experience.

I hope you will enjoy and use this book to an end of joyful food-related experiences in which you may find yourself. I have certainly enjoyed the journey. These recipes are tried and true. Many events have been enriched by the flavorful and fun ideas contained in this book and have been perfected over my many years of food service.

Remember that the main focus of any event should always be the people you are involved with—those whom we serve—not the food itself. Think of the people's needs, and all of your endeavors will be successful and rewarding for everyone involved.

Thanks for letting me be a part of your service opportunity.

Tips For Success

Food Safety

Food safety is, of course, very important. No event planner wants guests to go home feeling sick because of undercooked or incorrectly stored food. Keeping food at a proper temperature (below 40 degrees or above 140 degrees) during transportation needs to be considered during the planning process. Cleanliness of all food handlers should go without saying, but then I just said it, didn't I?

Getting Started

When you begin planning for your food preparation, remember that purchasing, storing, cooking, storing again, transporting, reheating, and serving food, and storing leftovers are all part of the process. Yes, there are many stages of food storage, and you will need to plan for each step.

Planning ahead simplifies and gives peace to your work. No matter how many details you think about, more will pop up as the larger details are put in place. So the earlier you plan, the more you can relax, and you will alleviate last-minute stresses or omissions. Part of planning ahead is finalizing the main details and then enlisting the help of others. Delegating responsibilities, so each person is in charge of a little piece of the big picture, makes large events easier on everyone and allows others to grow through their service.

> "Part of planning ahead is finalizing the main details and then enlisting the help of others."

The forms included in this book come from many years of experience, and by copying and using them, you will benefit from the lessons I learned through trial and error. There are so many details involved in a successful event, and these forms might help you remember some details you might have otherwise forgotten. These forms also inform those involved in the event of the details. The more people know, the more they can help. Get organized!

Purchasing Supplies

Some shopping strategies might help you stretch your budget to make your event more successful than you thought at the beginning. Some grocery stores will give unpublished discounts on large orders, for example on meat or produce. There have been times when I wanted to buy a cut of meat on sale that I wouldn't need for several weeks. So I asked the butcher if the store would consider giving me the same price on the same meat, and let me

> ## "Don't forget to ask for help!"

pick it up on a later date. Because I was ordering a large quantity, they agreed to that price. Buying produce by the case will sometimes reap the same reward. It's free to ask.

When you are shopping at the larger warehouse stores, never assume they will have all of an item you will need on the day you will need it. They will allow you to order what you want, which will guarantee you will have the amount you want. Other large supply houses will deliver for free if your order is large enough. This is particularly helpful if food items need refrigeration in transit.

Preparation

Preparing as much of the food in advance as possible, while never sacrificing quality, can save you work and stress on the day of the event. Preparations such as grating cheese, chopping vegetables, cooking meats that hold well (like ground beef), and making sauces and gravies can all be done a day or two ahead of time. There are often people who would love to help you with these preparations a day or two ahead but cannot help the day of the event. Don't forget to ask for help!

You Can Do This!

After you have been in charge of a few events, you will get better at all of these steps to success—and probably discover some of your own ideas. I hope that my experience and guidance will be of assistance to many and will make the work more enjoyable.

Event Planning

Event Name: _____

Organization: _____

Date and Time: _____

Location: _____

Attendees

Adults _____ Teenagers _____ Children _____ Leaders _____

Food Requirements *(Meals or refreshments)*

_____

_____

_____

Special Considerations: _____

Facilities

Reservations made to _____

Phone # _____ Event Date _____

Tables: Quantity _____ Size _____

Chairs _____

Set up

When _____   By whom _____

Take down

When _____   By whom _____

If event is not in a church building, you may need to check:

☐ Lighting & electrical outlet availability _____

☐ Bathroom facilities _____

☐ Garbage cans _____

☐ Garbage bags, if needed _____

☐ Parking availability _____

☐ Security deposit amount $ _____

                                             Due by date: _____

☐ Agreement/reservation in writing _____

☐ Dishwashing/cleanup facilities _____

☐ Bathrooms _____

☐ Backup if bad weather _____

Menu Plan

Many events will only require one meal, but some will offer more than one. You may be providing a lunch and a dinner or a breakfast and a lunch.

This form is helpful to use in organizing multiple courses for each meal and multiple meals, especially if individuals are supervising different meals. This will allow everyone to be clear on all of the details. Make as many copies of this form as needed for your event.

Meal: _____

Beverage: _____

Appetizer: _____

Soup or Salad: _____

Main Course: _____

Vegetable: _____

Side Dish: _____

Bread: _____

FOOD QUANTITIES

The amount of food you plan on purchasing is a delicate decision. You certainly don't want to run out, but you also don't want to have a lot of leftovers if you are working with someone else's budget. The amount of food needed can vary depending on the type of food served, the time of day, and the people attending.

The older a group is, the less they will probably eat. Teenage boys will eat more than teenage girls. Girls tend to like the sweets, boys tend to like the "meat-and-potatoes."

Consider the time of day. If you are serving a brunch or a lunch, people will eat more either because they haven't had breakfast, or they have worked up an appetite. If it is an evening event, and a meal is not being served, it is helpful to specify in the invitations that only refreshments will be served, so guests will have dinner before they arrive.

How the food is being served is also crucial to portion control. If you have a buffet line where guests can serve themselves, or if you might expect a second trip for some, consider planning for one and a half times the portion per guest. If you can control a one-time buffet trip, single portions will be fine. Some guests will take larger portions, some will take smaller portions, and some guests will skip some of the items altogether.

Serving time is cut down significantly if buffet tables can be set up for guests to go down both sides. However, if you are worried about running out of food, you can control portion size by having servers on one side of the table and guests on the other.

When serving desserts, it is helpful to have servers cut and place the portions onto plates. Even when cookies are being served, if they are all on a large platter, some guests will not be prudent. By placing one large cookie or two small cookies on napkins on the serving tables, you will let guests know what portion is expected. They may return as the crowd thins out, but this is a very successful way to make sure all guests receive "firsts."

For a sit-down dinner, where portions are equal in size and served to guests, plan on 10 percent extra for unexpected guests. It's always better to be safe than sorry.

If guests are expected to come and go quickly, less is needed. If they are staying around for hours, and food is available, they will usually eat more than one serving. This is especially true if the weather is hot because more beverages will be consumed throughout the event. Guests who don't want a sweetened beverage appreciate having ice water readily available.

PURCHASING & SUPPLIES

Purchasing Guide

	NUMBER OF SERVINGS				
	1	25	50	100	200
Appetizers	6	150	300	600	1200
Beverages					
Milk	8 oz.	1½ gal.	3 gal.	6 gal.	12 gal.
Juice	6 oz.	1 gal.	2 gal.	4 gal.	8 gal.
Soda					
for beverages	8 oz.	3 gal.	6 gal.	12 gal.	24 gal.
for floats	6 oz.	2 gal.	4 gal.	8 gal.	16 gal.
Punch	8 oz.	2½ gal.	5 gal.	10 gal.	20 gal.
Condiments					
Ketchup	1 Tbsp.	16 oz.	2 lbs.	4 lbs.	8 lbs.
Mustard	1 tsp.	5 oz.	10 oz.	20 oz.	40 oz.

Condiments (continued)	NUMBER OF SERVINGS				
	1	25	50	100	200
Mayonnaise	1 Tbsp.	13 oz.	26 oz.	52 oz.	104 oz.
Pickles	1 oz.	1 qt.	½ gal.	1 gal.	2 gal.
Salad Dressing	2 Tbsp.	25 oz.	3 lbs.	6 lbs.	12 lbs.
Dairy					
Butter	1 tsp.	¾ lb.	1½ lbs.	3 lbs.	6 lbs.
	1 Tbsp.	2¼ lbs.	4½ lbs.	9 lbs.	18 lbs.
Cheese					
grated	¼ cup	2 lbs..	4 lbs.	8 lbs.	16 lbs.
pre-sliced	$^2/_3$ oz.	1¼ lb.	2½ lbs.	5 lbs.	10 lbs.
Sour Cream	2 Tbsp.	28 oz.	3½ lbs.	7 lbs.	14 lbs.
Whipped Cream, *aerosol can*	2 Tbsp.	7 oz.	14 oz.	28 oz.	52 oz.
Cream, *to be whipped*	2 Tbsp.	1 pt.	2 pt.	4 pt.	8 pt.

Dessert	NUMBER OF SERVINGS				
	1	25	50	100	200
Whipped Topping, *frozen*	2 Tbsp.	8 oz.	16 oz.	32 oz.	64 oz.
Cake					
15 x 10 x 2 (cookie sheet)	2½-inch square	1 cake	2 cakes	4 cakes	8 cakes
9 x 13	2x3-inch piece	2 cakes	4 cakes	7 cakes	13 cakes
9 x 13	3x3-inch piece	3 cakes	5 cakes	9 cakes	17 cakes
10-inch cheesecake	$^1/_8$ cake	4 cakes	7 cakes	13 cakes	25 cakes
12-inch cheesecake	$^1/_{10}$ cake	3 cakes	5 cakes	10 cakes	20 cakes
14-inch cheesecake	$^1/_{16}$ cake	2 cakes	4 cakes	7 cakes	13 cakes
Ice cream	½ cup	3 qt.	6 qt.	4 gal.	8 gal.
Pie, 9-inch	$^1/_6$ pie	5 pies	9 pies	17 pies	34 pies
	$^1/_8$ pie	4 pies	7 pies	13 pies	25 pies

Meat		NUMBER OF SERVINGS			
	1	25	50	100	200
Beef					
roast	4 oz.	12 lbs.	25 lbs.	50 lbs.	100 lbs.
ground	3 oz. *(taco size)*	5 lbs.	10 lbs.	20 lbs.	40 lbs.
patty	4 oz.	6 lbs.	12 lbs.	24 lbs.	48 lbs.
Ham, *cooked*	4 oz.	10 lbs.	20 lbs.	40 lbs.	80 lbs.
Hot Dogs	2	50	100	200	400
Chicken					
whole	1 piece	3 whole	6 whole	12 whole	24 whole
boneless, skinless breast	$1/3$ lb.	8 lbs.	16 lbs.	32 lbs.	64 lbs.
Turkey					
whole	3 oz.	15 lbs.	30 lbs.	60 lbs.	120 lbs.
precooked	3 oz.	7 lbs.	14 lbs.	28 lbs.	56 lbs.

Rice & Pasta					
Rice, *cooked*	5 oz.	25 oz.	50 oz.	100 oz.	200 oz.
Pasta, *dry*	2 oz.	3 lbs.	6 lbs.	12 lbs.	24 lbs.

Sauces	NUMBER OF SERVINGS				
	1	25	50	100	200
Chocolate Sauce	2 Tbsp.	36 oz.	5 lbs.	10 lbs.	20 lbs.
Maple Syrup	¼ cup	50 oz.	3 qt.	6 qt.	12 qt.
Barbecue Sauce	2 Tbsp.	30 oz.	60 oz.	120 oz.	240 oz.
Spaghetti Sauce	½ cup	26 oz.	14 lbs.	28 lbs.	52 lbs.
Vegetables					
Carrots	2–3 sticks	1 lb.	2 lbs.	4 lbs.	8 lbs.
Celery	3-inch cut	2 lbs.	4 lbs.	8 lbs.	16 lbs.
Lettuce					
as condiment	1 leaf	1 head	2 heads	4 heads	8 heads
salad mix	¼ lb.	5 lbs.	10 lbs.	20 lbs.	40 lbs.
Potatoes					
whole	1	25	50	100	200
mashed, instant (*½-cup servings*)	1	25	50	100	200
Tomatoes	1 slice	3 lbs.	6 lbs.	12 lbs.	24 lbs.
Frozen Vegetables	$1/3$ cup	5 lbs.	10 lbs.	20 lbs.	40 lbs.
Canned Vegetables *#10 can, 6–7 lbs each*	½ cup	1 can	2 cans	4 cans	8 cans

MISCELLANEOUS TIPS

Appetizers: Each appetizer is 2–3 bites, 6 pieces per guest.

Dips: A serving is 3 oz. of dip or salsa per guest

Soups: A serving is 1 cup if soup is an appetizer. It is 2 cups if is a main dish.

Salad: Two or three large heads or 2 lbs. of green salad mix serves ten people; 1 cup of salad weighs about 3 oz.

Potatoes, rice, or pasta: A serving is about 5 oz.

Desserts: A serving is 1 piece of dessert if served while sitting, and 1½ if an open-table serving.

Hot dogs: Two hot dogs are 1 serving for teens and adults.

Punch: One gallon serves 10 guests, but if the weather is hot and event is long, double the amount provided.

SUPPLY CHECKLIST

Item	Type	Size	Quantity	Price	Buy From
Cups					
Plates					
Bowls					
Napkins					
Straws					
Knives					
Forks					
Spoons					
Aluminum Foil					
Zippered Bags					

Item	Type	Size	Quantity	Price	Buy From
Paper Towels					
Garbage Bags					
Tablecloths					
Ice					
Other					

THEMES

Spring Themes

Valentine's Day

- giant tissue paper flowers and hearts
- giant conversation hearts
- doilies, and heart shape foil doilies
- giant candy kisses made with aluminum foil *(empty)*

Luck o' the Irish

- chocolate gold coins
- four-leaf clovers
- derby hats
- rainbows
- pots of gold

No Foolin' (April Fools' Day)

Blooming Fun

- picket fence
- garden tools
- sunflowers
- large tissue-paper flowers
- Five oval balloons with a small round balloon in the center makes a great flower.

Signs of Spring

- cut-outs of lady bugs, bees, and other bugs
- caterpillars, one large red balloon *(with eyes)* and four green balloons for body
- baby birds made from paper
- red-checkered tablecloths
- balloon rainbow, made with ten balloons of six colors tied to one string
- daisies in glass soda bottles

Spring Refreshments

- vases filled with candy conversation hearts
- bird nests with coconut or chow mein and butterscotch chips with jelly beans
- root beer, apple beer, Irish cream sodas
- Twinkies sliced open with Twix *(hot dog; April Fools' Day)*
- pudding cups with crushed cookies and gummy worms on top

SUMMER THEMES

Under the Sea

- seaweed *(green streamers)*
- sand and sea shells in any glass container
- helium balloon bubbles
- sunken boat
- treasure chest

Surf's Up

- surfboards
- beach towels on walls or tables
- giant paper sunset on the wall with waves below
- beach umbrellas and chairs

Hawaiian Holiday

- palm trees *(made out of construction paper and carpet roll tubes)*
- brightly colored plastic tablecloths
- grass skirts
- Hawaiian leis
- tiki torches

Summer Splash

- pool toys
- brightly colored tablecloths
- lifeguard shirts

Summer Refreshments

- ice cream floats, use several flavors of ice cream and soda
- cake with candy dolphins on them
- snow cones or frozen slushies
- different flavored syrups in sodas
- banana splits or sundaes *(add your own toppings)*
- brownie sundae
- cookie ice cream sandwiches

FALL THEMES

Back to School

- chalkboards
- alphabet letters
- college pennants
- apples
- school supplies

Harvest Friends

- corn stalks
- bales of hay
- scarecrows
- apples and pumpkins

Pirate's Cove

- invitations that look like treasure maps
- swords, eye patches, head scarves
- ship's hull
- skeleton
- gold coins *(chocolate)* and beads

Caribbean Cruise

- port holes
- waves
- coconuts
- islands cut from brown paper
- fishing net
- seashells
- piña colada drinks

Halloween

- orange Chinese lanterns with painted jack-o'-lantern faces
- cheesecloth for spooky curtains
- tissue-paper wedding bells draped in cheesecloth with black eyes and mouths *(ghosts)*
- orange helium balloons for each guest to draw a face on
- giant paper black cats and bats
- large, multi-limbed branch in a pumpkin with paper bats hanging from it
- large candy corn candies cut from stiff paper
- witches' broomsticks: Take two brown sacks and cut slits in one all the way to the base. Put candy inside the uncut bag, then a stick. Draw the cut bag up around all side of the uncut bag and tie with yarn or twine.

Fall Refreshments

- apples *(e.g., apple crisp, caramel apples, hot apple cider, and so on)*
- donuts, decorate your own
- pumpkin cookies
- bowls of nuts
- candy corn cupcakes
- different types of flavored popcorn
- witches' hats: Turn a fudge-striped cookie upside down, use corn syrup to affix a candy kiss and add pipe a frosting bow
- Cupcakes with crushed chocolate cookies on top with bone candy sticking out

WINTER THEMES

Winter Wonderland

- handmade paper snowflakes or paper doilies *(coffee filters are perfect for this)*
- white helium filled balloons
- white Christmas lights, lots of them
- thin branches painted silver, with glitter

Snowman Village

- winter accessories, especially scarves
- white Chinese lanterns *(easy to store and reuse and redecorate)*
- paper mittens and top hats

Ice Magic

- wrap boxes in plastic or bubble wrap
- silver stars
- dry ice
- mirrors

Winter Sports

- sporting equipment, skis, snowshoes, hockey sticks, ice skates
- fluffy quilt batting *(looks like snow)*
- pictures of ski lift and other winter scenes
- medals made from frozen juice can lids and ribbon
- Five colored rings *(for Olympic logo)*

Winter Refreshments

- ice cream balls rolled in coconut, or cupcakes with coconut
- hot cider with whipped cream and nutmeg sprinkles
- hot chocolate, use candy cane for stirring
- white powdered donuts
- chocolate cupcakes with tiny marshmallows on top

MISCELLANEOUS THEMES

New Year's Eve & Prom Themes

- A Night at the Museum
- A Bright Tomorrow
- Glitter Galaxy
- Fifties
- A Night in Paris
- An Evening in Venice
- Star Quality
- Hollywood Premier
- Masquerade Ball
- Movie Magic
- Garden Splendor

- Castles in the Clouds
- Knights and Ladies
- Retro
- Disco Dancing
- Starry, Starry Nights
- Winter Wonderland
- Big City, Bright Lights
- A Night on the Nile
- New York, New York
- Top Hats and Tails

Anytime Themes

- Current TV Shows
- Current Music Trends
- Disco
- Rock On!
- Italian Vacation
- Black and White
- Techno-Robo
- Mexican Riviera
- Medieval Times
- World Series

- Outer Space
- Circus Spectacular
- Academy Awards
- New York City
- Time Square
- Superheroes
- Super Bowl
- World Cup

LARGE GROUP EVENTS

LARGE GROUPS: BUFFETS

When you are in charge of serving many people—quickly and on a budget—flavorful and plentiful hot food, it is important to first choose your menu and preparation methods.

One thing to remember is to keep the food choices flavorful yet generic. Or provide a way for guests to "personalize" the meal to their tastes. Leaving the choice of onions, dressings, and especially spicy things like salsa or peppers up to the individual will make more people happy with what they are eating.

Roasters and slow cookers are very helpful in preparing and serving hot foods. These are often easy to borrow and relatively inexpensive to buy, especially during the winter holiday season.

It is a challenge to serve food in a buffet line and keep it hot until guests sit down to eat. Since most buildings do not allow open flames, such as those used in warming tables, heating possibilities are limited. Serving foods already in a sauce or gravy can help keep the food hot longer. Offering hot foods and main dishes last on the buffet line assists in that goal and can cut down on people overfilling their plates with the main course, causing you to run low on that item.

When serving drinks, it is helpful to have a separate table for drinks away from the main buffet line. Often guests will want to return to the drink table, and keeping it separate from the buffet line allows them to grab another drink without getting back in line. It is also a good way to serve dessert, much like at a wedding.

The larger the plate provided, the more food they will take on their initial visit. We often fill our plates when much less will fill our stomachs. Using a reasonably sized plate is sufficient, but if return trips are allowed, you need to plan to have extra plates. This also holds true for cups. Placing the napkins and silverware at the end of the table or at the drink table is more convenient for guests. If they pick these up at the beginning of the line, they will be fumbling with them while trying to get food.

Some of the most successful buffets are those that are "bars," such as a potato bar or a salad bar. This allows guests to build the meal of their choice and be pleased with their individual meals.

"BUILD-A-MEAL" BUFFET IDEAS

Large Groups

- **baked potato bar**
  baked potatoes, chili, variety of
  grated cheese, onions, bacon,
  tomatoes, broccoli, sour cream

- **barbecue beef sandwich**
  onions, cheese, tomatoes

- **barbecue chicken sandwiches**
  add coleslaw and onions

- **breakfast burrito bar**
  eggs, cheeses, lettuce, sour cream,
  onions, mushrooms, hot sauce,
  potato chunks, tortillas

- **burrito bar**
  beans, cheeses, meat, lettuce, sour
  cream, onions, salsa, guacamole,
  tortillas

- **build-a-burger bar**
  meat (regular, veggie, and turkey
  burgers), cheeses, lettuce, onions,
  tomatoes, pickles, buns, condiments

- **chili bar**
  onions, sour cream, cheeses, peppers, tomatoes

- **Hawaiian Haystacks** (see p. 50)

- **hot dog bar**
  hot dogs, buns, condiments,
  cheese, chili, onions

- **nacho bar**
  cheese, chips, beans, lettuce, peppers, onions, salsa, sour cream

- **pasta bar**
  one type of pasta, several choices
  of sauces (e.g., meat sauce, alfredo
  sauce) and toppings (e.g. cheese)

- **salad bar**
  lettuce, spinach, sprouts, cheeses,
  tomatoes, onions, celery, cucum-
  bers, radishes, mushrooms, grated
  carrots, hard-boiled eggs, beets,
  sesame seeds, sunflower seeds,
  bacon bits, chopped nuts, and so on

- **soup bar**
  variety of soup, onions, sour cream,
  cheeses, croutons

- **taco salad bar**
  seasoned ground beef, lettuce,
  tomatoes, cheese, onions, sour
  cream, mild and hot taco sauces

- **taco soup bar**
  meat in sauce, chips, cheese,
  lettuce, sour cream, guacamole,
  olives, tomatoes

SYDNEY CLINE   29

Cheese Ball Appetizers

{Makes 100–120}

3 lbs. cream cheese
2 lbs. mozzarella cheese, finely grated
2 lbs. cheddar cheese, finely grated
2 cups finely chopped walnuts

Place cream cheese in large bowl.

Add other cheeses gradually and knead with a fork.

When all of cheeses are added, knead mixture with hands until all cheeses are combined.

Take a teaspoon or so of the mixture, roll into a ball, roll in chopped nuts, and refrigerate.

Serve with a variety of crackers.

Variations: Add bacon bits or finely chopped green onions to the mixture. (I don't add onions if I am serving a lot of people, since some don't like onions.) Or divide mixture into thirds and add different seasonings to each part.

Note:
These can be made days ahead of your event and stored in zippered plastic bags.

Cheesy Spinach Squares

{Makes 24 mini or 9–12 large servings}

½ cup butter
3 eggs
1 cup flour
1 tsp. salt

1 tsp. baking powder
1 cup milk
4 cups grated Monterey Jack cheese
4 cups fresh chopped spinach

Melt butter in 9x13 baking dish.

Beat eggs.

Mix flour, salt, and baking powder in a separate bowl.

Add eggs to flour mixture, but do not overmix.

Stir in spinach and cheese.

Spread mixture into dish.

Bake at 350 degrees for 30–35 minutes. Cut into squares.

Serve hot, or freeze and reheat when you want to serve them.

Note:
Use a 12x18 cookie sheet with sides for a double recipe.
These travel well.

Jack Cheese Green Chili Toasts

{Makes 16–20}

1 loaf sliced sourdough or french bread *(16–20 slices)*
2 (4-oz.) cans chopped green chilies
1 Tbsp. butter
4 cups grated Monterey Jack cheese
4 Tbsp. mayonnaise

Melt butter.
Add butter to chilies and stir well.
Place sliced bread on cookie sheet.
Spread chili mixture onto bread.
Mix mayonnaise with cheese.
Cover chili mixture with cheese mixture.
Broil these for 2 minutes to lightly toast.
Serve warm.

Exotic Fruit Cup Variations

Tropical Fresh Fruit Cups

{Makes about 50}

1 medium watermelon, scooped into balls
1 lb. green grapes
2 cantaloupes, cubed
3–4 bananas, sliced
1 medium pineapple, sliced, then wedged

shredded coconut *(optional)*
4 cups piña colada or vanilla yogurt
4 cups sour cream
granola or granola-based breakfast cereal
clear plastic cups *(4–6 oz.)*

Cut up fruit, each type in a specific shape, if possible.

Mix yogurt with sour cream.

Stir yogurt into fruit, coating well.

Keep refrigerated.

Put fruit into small, clear cups and sprinkle a little granola on top.

Note:
Add bananas as close to serving as possible.
Yogurt helps keep bananas from browning too quickly.

Super Simple Fruit Cups

{Makes about 50}

1 (#10) can fruit cocktail
1 (#10) can sliced peaches
1 (16-oz.) pkg. small marshmallows

1 (16-oz.) pkg. small marshmallows
6–8 bananas, sliced
clear plastic cups *(4–6 oz.)*

Drain fruit cocktail and peaches.

Mix in marshmallows and bananas.

Keep refrigerated.

Serve in small, clear cups for easy buffet line flow and portion control.

Mandarin-Coconut Fruit Cups

{Makes about 50}

3 (11-oz.) cans mandarin oranges
1 (20-oz.) can pineapple chunks
1 (16-oz.) container lemon or vanilla yogurt

1 (10-oz.) pkg. small marshmallows
1 cup shredded coconut
clear plastic cups *(4–6 oz.)*

Drain mandarin oranges and pineapple chunks.

Mix all ingredients.

Keep refrigerated.

Serve in small, clear cups.

Notes:
Fruit can be cut up quite far in advance and kept refrigerated.
Variety is the key to pleasing many guests.

Nut Cups

{Makes about 50}

mixed nuts
peanuts
cashews
clear plastic cups *(4–6 oz.)*

Fill small, clear cups with either one type of nut or a mixture and serve.

Veggie Cups

{Makes about 50}

carrot sticks
celery sticks
slices of colorful peppers
ranch dip, nacho cheese, or salad dressing *(or any other mild, creamy dip)*
clear plastic cups *(4–6 oz.)*

Place about 2 tablespoons of dip into each clear plastic cup.

Cut carrots, peppers, and celery into sticks long enough to extend 2 inches above rim of cups.

Serve immediately or refrigerate for up to 30 minutes

Note:

Make some with carrots only, celery only, or a mixture of vegetables. This makes a colorful, healthy, quick-to-serve option for appetizers.

Easiest Meatballs and Sauce Ever!

{Makes about 50}

2 (16-oz.) jars grape jelly
2 (12-oz.) bottle chili sauce
2 lbs. frozen meatballs *(about 50)*

Mix jelly and chili sauce.
Pour over meatballs and heat slowly.
Serve with toothpicks.

Note:
This is a favorite for weddings, appetizers, and side dishes.
The taste is far beyond the parts of the whole.

Honey-Glazed Carrots

{Makes 50 servings}

7 lbs. carrots
1½ cups butter
1½ cups honey
½ cup orange juice
⅓ cup fresh parsley

Peel carrots if not using baby carrots.

Fill stockpot ¾ full with salted water.

Bring water to boil, add carrots, and parboil until tender. Do not overcook.

Melt butter in a saucepan over low heat.

Add honey and orange juice to saucepan and bring to a boil over medium heat.

Add honey mixture to warm carrots. Toss to coat.

Toss in parsley and add salt and pepper to taste.

Keep warm in roaster or covered aluminum pan in the oven at 250 degrees.

Note:
Once boiled, carrots can be refrigerated for up to one day.

Dinner Yams for 50

{Makes 50 servings}

butter for greasing pans
5 (28.5-oz.) cans yams
3 cups brown sugar
1 cup butter, cut into ½-inch pieces

Preheat oven to 350 degrees.

Butter all sides of two 9x13 pans or one 12x18 pan.

Cut yams into portion sizes for uniform cooking.

Place yams in pans.

Sprinkle with brown sugar.

Distribute butter evenly over yams.

Cover with foil.

Bake 30 minutes.

Remove foil and bake 15–20 minutes longer, or until yams are tender and slightly caramelized.

Hawaiian Sweet Potatoes

{Makes 8 servings}

6–8 medium sweet potatoes
½ tsp. salt
¼ cup butter, melted
1 (20-oz.) can crushed pineapple and juice
¼ cup brown sugar
1 tsp. nutmeg
1 tsp. cinnamon

{Makes 40 servings}

35 medium-sized sweet potatoes
2½ tsp. salt
1¼ cup butter, melted
1 (100-oz.) can crushed pineapple and juice
1¼ cup brown sugar
5 tsp. nutmeg
5 tsp. cinnamon

Wash sweet potatoes well.

Cook sweet potatoes on low boil until medium done, not soft.

Let potatoes cool. Then peel and slice them, and put in a slow cooker.

Mix remaining ingredients in a bowl and pour over sweet potatoes.

Cover and cook on high for about 4 hours.

Note:
This recipe is cooked slow and stays hot.

Mashed Potatoes for 50

{Makes 50 servings}

25 lbs. russet potatoes
1½ lbs. butter
2 cups heavy cream
salt and pepper to taste

Wash, peel, and cube potatoes.

Place potatoes in large stockpot of warm water, bring to boil, and boil until tender. *(Do not over boil.)*

Whip potatoes with butter and heavy cream until light and fluffy.

Add salt and pepper to taste.

Keep warm in roaster or covered aluminum pan in a 250-degree oven.

Fiesta Spanish Rice

{Makes 10 servings}

¼ cup vegetable oil
¼ cup chopped yellow onion
3 cups cooked white rice
4 cups chicken broth
2 cups mild chunky salsa

{Makes 50 servings}

1¼ cup vegetable oil
1¼ cup chopped yellow onion
15 cups cooked white rice
20 cups chicken broth
10 cups mild chunky salsa

Heat oil in a large skillet over medium heat and sauté.

Mix in cooked rice, stirring often until lightly browned.

Add chicken broth and salsa.

Reduce heat to low, cover pan, and simmer for 20 minutes.

Remove from heat and serve.

Island Pulled Pork

{Makes 8 servings}

3 lbs. boneless rolled pork loin roast
1 (16-oz.) can jellied cranberry sauce
½ cup white sugar
½ cup cranberry juice or cranberry cocktail
1 tsp. dry mustard
¼ tsp. ground cloves

2 Tbsp. cornstarch
2 Tbsp. cold water
salt to taste

Place roast in a slow cooker set on low.

Combine cranberry sauce, sugar, cranberry juice, mustard, and cloves in a separate bowl and pour over meat.

Cover and cook on low 6–8 hours.

Turn off cooker. Reserve juices in another pan.

Measure 2 cups reserved juices, adding water if necessary. In a saucepan, bring liquid to boil over medium heat. Combine cornstarch and cold water to make a paste. Stir into gravy. Cook and stir until thickened. Add salt to taste.

Serve over rice or as a pulled pork sandwich.

Note:
Add pineapple chunks prior to serving for a Hawaiian flare.
Or you could double the gravy portions, if you like extra gravy–I do!

Down-South Barbecue Chicken Sandwiches

{Makes 100}

100 lbs. whole chickens, cut up
19 cups ketchup
10 cups prepared mustard
4 cups brown sugar
4 cups minced garlic
4 cups honey

4 cups steak sauce
4 cups lemon juice
2½ cups liquid smoke flavoring
salt and pepper to taste
100 large hamburger buns
50 cups coleslaw

Place chicken in a large pot or roaster with enough water to cover. Bring to a boil and cook until chicken comes off the bone easily, about 3 hours. When chicken is done, remove all meat from bones, and chop or shred into small pieces. Discard skin and bones.

Make sauce. In a large stockpot, combine ketchup, mustard, brown sugar, garlic, honey, steak sauce, lemon juice, and liquid smoke. Season with salt and pepper. Bring mixture to a gentle boil over medium heat and let simmer for about 10 minutes. Set aside to allow flavors to mingle. This can be made several days ahead and refrigerated.

Pour sauce over cooked chicken prior to serving and mix well. Allow to heat for at least 15 minutes to allow the flavor of the sauce to soak into the meat. This holds very well and does not overcook. Be careful to keep chicken refrigerated (below 40 degrees) or warm (above 140 degrees) at all times.

Spoon barbecue chicken onto buns and top with coleslaw, if desired. (Coleslaw sauce should be light and mixed with cabbage just before serving.) This goes well with baked beans and applesauce or apples, and lemonade or root beer.

Great and Simple Beef Sandwiches

{Makes 8}

2–3 lb. chuck roast, cubed
1 pkg. dry onion soup mix
1 (12-oz.) can of cola
8 hamburger buns

{Makes 50}

16–18 lbs. chuck roast, cubed
6 pkgs. dry onion soup mix
1 two-liter bottle of cola
50 hamburger buns

Place meat in slow cooker or roaster.

Sprinkle soup mix over meat.

Pour cola over all.

Cover and cook on low for 8–10 hours.

Shred and serve as sandwiches, or serve as roast with potatoes and carrots.

Creamy Italian Chicken Breasts

{Makes 8–10 servings}

6–8 boneless, skinless chicken breasts
1 (0.7-oz.) pkg. dry Italian dressing mix
¾ cup diced onions
1 Tbsp. butter
1 (8-oz.) pkg. cream cheese
1 (10.75-oz.) can cream of chicken soup

{Makes 50 servings}

12–15 lbs. chicken breasts
5 (0.7-oz.) pkgs. dry Italian dressing mix
3¾ cups diced onions
5 Tbsp. butter
5 (8-oz.) pkgs. cream cheese
5 (10.75-oz.) cans cream of chicken soup

Place chicken, frozen or thawed, in a slow cooker *(or roaster for larger sizes).*

Sprinkle with dry Italian dressing mix.

Cook on low for 4–5 hours on high or 9–10 hours on low. *(Do not add liquid.)*

One hour before serving:

Sauté onions in butter in a saucepan over medium heat.

Add cream cheese and chicken soup concentrate.

Cook and stir until soupy.

Pour soup mixture over the chicken and cook for one more hour.

Note:

This recipe holds really well without becoming overdone. It also holds it's heat when served. Serve over rice, pasta, or mashed potatoes.

Hawaiian Haystacks Buffet

{Makes 100–125 servings}

chicken gravy mix, enough to make 3–4 gal. *(canned chicken gravy, or mix 12 [26-oz.] cans cream of chicken soup with 14 [14-oz.] cans of chicken broth)*

30 lbs. chicken breasts, cooked *(can be marinated in Italian salad dressing overnight and then cooked and chopped into bite-size pieces)*

3 boxes instant rice *(each box serves 35)*, cooked according to box directions

Toppings:

- chopped broccoli: about 10 lbs., steamed
- shredded carrots: about 5 lbs.
- chopped green onions: 3–4 bunches
- chopped celery: 3 whole heads
- shredded cheese: about 7 lbs.
- raisins: about 2 lbs.
- pineapple tidbits: 2 (#10) cans
- coconut: 1 lb., shredded
- chow mein noodles: 3–4 large cans
- Peanuts, salted: 2 (3-lbs. 8-oz.) containers

Note:
Make a buffet line and let people choose which toppings they want.
This is such a fun dish!

Scrambled Eggs Buffet

{Makes 50–75 servings}

100 eggs
8 tsp. salt
10 cups milk
4 cups butter

Beat eggs well.

Heat milk and salt slowly together in large pot over low heat.

Add eggs and butter to milk, but *do not stir*.

Place mixture in large roaster and cover.

Bake at 350 degrees for 30 minutes, then stir.

Bake another 30 minutes, stir, and serve immediately.

Alternate Baking Method

Divide butter among four 9x13 dishes. Combine eggs and salt. Mix well. Gradually add milk. Pour into the 4 pans. Bake, uncovered, at 350 degrees for 10 minutes. Stir. Bake 10–15 minutes more, or until done. Serve immediately.

Note:
You can stir in 2 pounds of cooked chopped ham or bacon after eggs have cooked for the first 30 minutes.

Everybody Loves Taco Soup

{Makes 12 large servings}

2 lbs. ground beef
1 (26.5-oz.) can spaghetti sauce
1 (15-oz.) can tomato sauce
1 (1.25-oz.) pkg. taco seasoning
1–2 cups water *(some like it soupier)*
1 (15-oz.) can diced tomatoes *(optional)*
1 (15-oz.) can kidney beans, rinsed *(optional)*

{Makes 50 large servings}

8 lbs. ground beef
4 (26.5-oz.) cans spaghetti sauce
4 (15-oz.) cans tomato sauce
4 (1.25-oz.) pkgs. taco seasoning
4–8 cups water
4 (15-oz.) cans diced tomatoes *(optional)*
4 (15-oz.) cans kidney beans, rinsed *(optional)*

Brown ground beef in a large pan over medium heat and drain fat.

Add spaghetti sauce, tomato sauce, water, and seasonings to meat.

Heat for 3–4 minutes.

Add diced tomatoes and kidney beans, if desired, and heat again.

Serve over with tortilla chips, if desired, and top with choice of toppings.

Choice of toppings:

onions, chopped
lettuce, shredded
tomatoes, chopped

black olives, sliced
sour cream
guacamole

cheddar cheese, grated
tortilla chips

SERVING ADULTS

Saucy Crab Dip (Faux Pizza)

{Makes 12–18 servings}

2 (8-oz.) pkgs. cream cheese

½–1 tsp. hot sauce *(depending on heat desired)*

2 tsp. lemon juice

1 jar chili sauce *(tastes like cocktail sauce)*

5 oz. crab *(cooked crab or imitation crab)*

fresh parsley

black olives *(optional)*

chopped green onions *(optional)*

Mix cream cheese, hot sauce, and lemon juice until creamy.

Spread cream cheese mixture on a 12- or 14-inch plate to about ½ inch from the edge.

Spread the chili sauce to about ½ inch from the edge of cream cheese.

Flake crab and sprinkle onto chili sauce.

Add any optional toppings.

Serve immediately with crackers, or chill and reheat just before serving.

Cran-Nutty Warm Brie

{Makes 10–12 servings}

⅓ cup dried cranberries
1 Tbsp. brown sugar
1 Tbsp. butter
2 Tbsp. slivered almonds, chopped pecans, or walnuts
1 (8-oz.) pkg. Brie cheese, softened at room temperature

Combine cranberries, brown sugar, butter, and nuts in a small bowl.

Microwave 30 seconds until butter melts.

Stir to blend all ingredients.

Cut Brie in half horizontally.

Put half of nutty mixture in the middle of cheese and half on top.

Microwave again for 45–60 seconds on high until cheese is soft and warm.

Serve with apple slices, crackers, or chunks of sourdough bread.

Petite Puffs

{Makes about 40}

½ cup butter
1 cup flour
¼ tsp. salt
4 eggs

Bring one cup of water to a boil, add butter, and boil until melted.

Add flour and salt and stir well.

Cook and stir over medium heat until mix forms a ball. *(It will start to look like children's play dough.)* Remove from heat.

Add eggs one at a time, beating after each egg to incorporate it.

Drop by teaspoonfuls onto a greased cookie sheet, 3 inches apart.

Bake at 450 degrees for 15 minutes, reduce heat to 325 degrees, and bake for an additional 20 minutes.

Remove puffs from oven and slice in half horizontally.

Turn oven off and return puffs to oven to dry for about 15 minutes.

Cool puffs on a rack.

Use immediately, refrigerate, or freeze until ready for use.

When ready to serve, fill each with your favorite chicken or turkey salad, or use the **Chicken Salad Petite Puff Filling** recipe on page 58.

Chicken Salad Petite Puff Filling

{Makes about 40 servings}

1 (10-oz.) can white chicken
1 Tbsp. mayonnaise
¼ cup chopped water chestnuts
¼ cup chopped celery
¼ cup green onions
1 tsp. seasoned salt

Drain chicken.

Put chicken in a bowl and break it up with a fork.

Add all other ingredients and mix well.

Chill.

Fill puffs just before serving.

Cottage Cheese Veggie Dip

{Makes about 4 cups}

2 cups cream-style cottage cheese
1 (8-oz.) pkg. soft cream cheese with onions and chives added
dill weed to garnish *(optional)*

Drain cottage cheese and discard liquid.

Combine cottage cheese and cream cheese with wooden spoon.

Refrigerate until ready to serve.

Top with dill weed, if desired.

Serve with vegetable pieces, crackers, or pita chips.

Tangy Cocktail Wieners

{Makes 8 servings}

1 lb. mini smoked cocktail wieners *(smokies)*
¼ cup orange marmalade
1 cup barbecue sauce

Combine smokies with barbecue sauce in a large bowl.

Heat barbecue sauce with smokies in a medium pan over medium heat until meat is warm.

Slowly stir in marmalade.

Serve warm.

Cream-alicious Spinach Dip

{Makes about 4 cups}

1 (8-oz.) pkg. cream cheese
½ (10-oz.) pkg. frozen chopped spinach, thawed and drained
2 cups mayonnaise
1 tsp. seasoned salt
1 Tbsp. chopped chives
½ cup heavy cream

Mix all ingredients in a blender.

Chill.

Serve with raw vegetables or crackers.

ADULT BRUNCH ASSORTMENT

BLT Wraps

{Makes 6 wraps or can be cut into 24 two-inch appetizers}

⅓ cup mayonnaise
6 (8- or 10-inch) flour tortillas
8 slices cooked bacon, crumbled
1 large tomato, sliced
2 cups shredded lettuce
1½ cups shredded cheddar cheese

Spread tortilla with mayonnaise.

Layer remaining ingredients on top.

Roll into a cone shape and secure with a toothpick.

Serve cold.

Sandwiches

{Prepare one per person}

Pita Pocket Sandwiches

Cut pita bread in half and fill with a leaf of lettuce and chicken or tuna salad.

Croissant Sandwiches

Make these with croissants, lunchmeat, tomato slices, cheese, lettuce, and mayonnaise.

Note:
For variation, use sprouts instead of lettuce and creamy bacon or buttermilk dressing instead of mayonnaise.

West Coast Apricot Chicken Quarters

{Makes 50}

50 chicken quarters, skinned
1 (6-lb. 9-oz.) can apricot halves in light syrup
2 cups chopped green onions
8 (12-oz.) pkgs. chicken bouillon *(or about ⅓ cup)*
½ cup orange juice concentrate, thawed

½ cup reduced-sodium soy sauce
10 Tbsp. butter, melted
1½ tsp. pepper

Preheat oven to 350 degrees.

Arrange chicken quarters in a single layer in six 9x13 or four 12x18 baking pans.

Combine in a medium bowl apricots and their syrup with green onions, bouillon, orange juice, soy sauce, butter, and pepper.

Pour apricot mixture over chicken.

Bake 1 hour 15 minutes, basting occasionally, until chicken is tender.

Crescent Roll Chicken Pillows

{Makes 12–24 servings}

1 (8-oz.) pkg. cream cheese

¼ cup butter

2 Tbsp. minced dry onions

2 cups cooked or canned chicken, chopped

1 small can chopped mushrooms

3 (12-count) pkgs. refrigerated crescent rolls

3 (12-count) pkgs. refrigerated crescent rolls

1 cup seasoned bread crumbs

½ cup melted butter

1 (10.75-oz.) can cream of chicken or mushroom soup

Cream together cream cheese and butter until soft.

Add onion, chicken, and mushrooms to mixture and mix thoroughly.

Separate and flatten crescent roll dough.

Put a spoonful of chicken mixture in each roll and fold into a triangular pillow shape. Pinch edges closed.

Dip each roll in melted butter and then in bread crumbs, covering both sides.

Bake at 350 degrees for 20 minutes. (If frozen, bake for 30 minutes, or until golden brown.)

Make the gravy by mixing soup with 1 can of milk while the pillows are baking. Heat and serve with the pillows.

Serve over or with rice. Once dipped in butter and bread crumbs, these refrigerate or freeze well to be baked at a later time.

Tangy Honey-Lime Chicken Enchiladas

{Makes 5 servings}

3 boneless, skinless chicken breasts
1 can green enchilada sauce *(size of can depends on how much sauce you like)*
4 cups mozzarella cheese, grated
sour cream
10–12 (10-inch) flour tortillas

Marinade
5 Tbsp. honey
½ Tbsp. chili powder
5 Tbsp. lime juice
1 tsp. garlic powder, or minced garlic

Cook and shred chicken.

Combine all ingredients for marinade and pour over chicken. Let stand at least 30 minutes or marinate in refrigerator overnight for a stronger flavor.

Pour ½ cup of enchilada sauce into 9x13 pan.

Roll up flour tortillas with a little of the chicken, a dollop of sour cream, cheese, and 1 tablespoon enchilada sauce.

Place them into pan and drizzle remaining sauce and a little cheese on top.

Bake at 350 degrees until lightly brown, about 30 minutes.

Serve with black beans, pico de gallo, and Spanish rice.

Orange-Glazed Carrots

{Makes 6 servings}

2 lbs. baby carrots

½ cup brown sugar

½ cup orange juice

3 Tbsp. butter or margarine

¾ tsp. cinnamon

¼ tsp. nutmeg

2 Tbsp. cornstarch

¼ cup water

{Makes 50 servings}

16 lbs. baby carrots

4 cups brown sugar

4 cups orange juice

¾ lb. butter or margarine

2 Tbsp. cinnamon

2 tsp. nutmeg

1 cup cornstarch

2 cups water

Place all ingredients except cornstarch and water into a slow cooker or roaster.

Cover and cook on low for 3–4 hours until tenderly crisp. Do not overcook.

Turn off the heat source.

Drain juices from carrots into a saucepan. Bring to a boil over medium heat.

Mix cornstarch and cold water in a bowl until blended well.

Pour cornstarch mixture slowly, while stirring, into juices, and boil for one minute until thick, stirring constantly to avoid lumps.

Pour over carrots and serve or refrigerate carrots for up to 24 hours. Reheat before serving.

Easy Cheesy Restaurant Drop Biscuits

{Makes 10–12 biscuits}

2 cups dry biscuit mix
⅔ cup milk
½ cup grated cheddar cheese
¼ cup butter, melted
(Optional: add ¼ tsp garlic powder to melted butter.)

Preheat oven to 450 degrees.

Mix biscuit mix, milk, and cheese in a bowl until moist.

Drop by spoonful onto an ungreased cookie sheet.

Bake 8–10 minutes, or until lightly brown.

Remove from oven and immediately brush with butter.

Note:
These can be reheated in the microwave.

Sour Cream Baked Potato Sauce

{Makes 16 one-tablespoon servings}

1 cup sour cream
2 Tbsp. real bacon bits
chives
1 tsp. lemon juice
1 tsp. barbecue seasoning

Mix ingredients and refrigerate.

Serve in place of butter and sour cream over baked potatoes.

Classy Chicken Cordon Bleu Soup

{Makes 8–10 one-cup servings}

6 Tbsp. butter

1 cup flour

2 cloves garlic, minced

6 Tbsp. butter

8 cups milk

4 cups grated swiss cheese

1½ cups cooked and cubed chicken

8 oz. thinly sliced ham, cut into small squares

2 (10.75-oz.) cans cream of chicken soup

salt and pepper to taste

Melt butter in a large saucepan over medium heat.

Whisk in flour and garlic. Let cook 2 minutes.

Whisk in cold milk slowly and bring to a boil, stirring constantly. Mixture will thicken as it boils.

Turn heat to low and add cheese. Stir until cheese is melted.

Add chicken, ham, soup, and salt and pepper to taste. Heat thoroughly.

Serve with sour cream, if desired.

No-Bake Cookie Dough Truffles

{Makes about 100}

¾ cup brown sugar

1 cup butter, softened at room temperature

1 tsp. vanilla

2 cups flour

1 can sweetened condensed milk

1 cup chopped pecans or walnuts

½ cup mini semisweet chocolate chips

2 cups chocolate chips, for dipping

Cream together brown sugar and butter.

Add flour, vanilla, and milk to mixture, and cream well.

Mix in nuts and mini chocolate chips.

Dip your hands in flour. Roll dough to make walnut-sized balls.

Place the balls on wax paper on a cookie tray.

Refrigerate about 2 hours.

Use a double boiler or microwave to slowly melt 2 cups of chocolate chips.

Dip balls in chocolate, return them to the wax paper and let set in refrigerator.

Decadent (but Easy) Chocolate Truffles

{Makes about 40}

1 (16-oz.) pkg. chocolate sandwich cookies, divided
1 (8-oz.) pkg. cream cheese, softened
2 (8-oz.) pkgs. semisweet baking chocolate, melted

Use a food processor or a zippered plastic bag and rolling pin to crush 9 cookies to fine crumbs; reserve for later use.

Crush remaining cookies to fine crumbs; place in medium bowl. Add cream cheese; mix until well blended. Roll cookie mixture into 40 balls, about 1-inch in diameter.

Dip balls in melted chocolate and place on wax paper on baking sheet. Sprinkle with reserved cookie crumbs.

Refrigerate until firm, about 1 hour. Cover leftover truffles and store in refrigerator.

Directions for melting chocolate: To melt chocolate in a microwave, put the chocolate in a bowl or mug. Set microwave to 50 percent power. Microwave in 30-second increments, stirring after each heating cycle. When chocolate begins to melt, microwave for smaller time increments—20 seconds, then 10, and even 5 at a time may be enough. Watch carefully because chocolate can burn easily. Stir well at the end. The heat within the chocolate will continue to melt any remaining lumps as you stir. Do not overheat.

> *Note:*
> After dipping, any leftover chocolate can be stored at room temperature for another use.

Delectable Éclair Bars

{Makes 18 large or 24 small servings}

1 cup water
½ cup butter
1 cup flour
4 eggs
2 small pkgs. instant vanilla pudding mix *(4 cups of canned pudding can be substituted for instant pudding and milk.)*
2½ cups milk
1 (8-oz.) pkg. cream cheese
1 tsp. vanilla
1 (8-oz.) container frozen whipped topping
chocolate syrup, cocoa powder, fresh berries for garnish *(optional)*

Bring water and butter to a boil in a medium saucepan over medium heat.

Remove from heat and dump all flour in at once. Stir until it forms a ball.

Let stand to cool 10 minutes.

Beat eggs into mixture one at a time using a fork.

Spray a 12x18 cookie sheet (with sides) lightly with cooking spray.

Spread dough to the edges of the pan.

Bake 30 minutes at 425 degrees. Poke holes in any bubbles that occur while baking.

Let crust cool completely. (May be refrigerated for a day or so, if needed)

Combine pudding and milk (or canned pudding), vanilla, and cream cheese.

(At this point you can refrigerate this mixture for a day or so, if desired, and assemble the éclairs just prior to serving. This also makes it very easy to transport!)

Spread pudding mixture onto cooled crust.

Spread whipped topping on top of pudding mixture.

Drizzle with chocolate syrup, dust with cocoa powder if desired, and serve with a few raspberries or a large strawberry.

Note:
Be sure to have copies of this recipe on hand when you serve it.
Everyone will want a copy!

Chilled Berry Smoothie No-Bake Cheesecake

{Makes one 9x13 pan, or 12–16 servings}

Crust
1½ cups graham cracker crumbs
¼ cup butter, melted
2 Tbsp. sugar

Filling
4 (8-oz.) pkgs. cream cheese, softened
½ cup sugar
1 pkg. frozen mixed berries, thawed, drained, and smashed
1 (8-oz.) tub whipped topping *(3 cups)*

Spray a 9x13 pan with cooking spray or line with aluminum foil for easy cutting and serving.

Combine graham cracker crumbs, butter, and sugar and press into pan.

Beat together cream cheese and ½ cup sugar in a large bowl.

Stir berries into cream cheese mixture.

Fold in 2 cups of whipped topping gently, reserving 1 cup.

Spoon mixture onto crust.

Cover and refrigerate at least 4 hours.

Top with leftover cup of whipped topping before serving.

Lemon Cheesecake Squares

{Makes one 9x13 pan, or 12–16 servings}

Crust

1 sleeve *(9 crackers)* graham crackers, crushed

½ cup butter, melted

1 Tbsp. sugar

Filling

1 (3-oz.) box lemon gelatin mix

3 (8-oz.) pkgs. cream cheese

1 cup sugar

2 Tbsp. vanilla extract

1 (12-oz.) can evaporated milk

Combine cracker crumbs, butter, and sugar in a medium bowl.

Coat a 9x13 baking dish with cooking spray.

Line the pan with the cracker mixture, reserving ¼ cup of crumbs.

Add gelatin mix to one cup of boiling water and stir to dissolve. Let cool.

Cream together cream cheese and sugar in a medium bowl.

Mix in milk, vanilla, and cooled gelatin slowly. Then beat when incorporated, until smooth.

Pour filling over crumb crust.

Sprinkle with remaining crumbs.

Refrigerate until firm, 8–24 hours before serving.

Raspberry Sauce

{Makes 1¼ cups or 18 one-tablespoon servings}

1 (10-oz.) pkg. frozen raspberries in syrup, thawed
3 Tbsp. sugar
1 tsp. cornstarch

Use a food processor or blender to mix raspberries with syrup until smooth. If desired, use a strainer to remove seeds.

Combine sugar and cornstarch in a small saucepan.

Stir in raspberry puree.

Cook over medium heat until mixture boils and thickens.

Cool and store in the refrigerator.

Serve with chocolate cake or with **Lemon Cheesecake Squares** (found on p. 79).

Frozen Fudge Sundae Dessert

{Makes one 9x13 pan, or 12–16 servings}

Crust
24 chocolate sandwich cookies
¼ cup melted butter

Ice cream layer
½ gallon vanilla ice cream, softened
½ cup chopped walnuts, almonds, or pecans

Fudge Layer
½ cup butter
2 cups powdered sugar
1 (12-oz.) can evaporated milk
8 oz. semisweet chocolate chips

Chop the cookies with a large knife to medium-fine crumb (or chop in food processor).

Add butter to cookies and stir well.

Press cookie mixture firmly into the bottom of a 9x13 baking dish and freeze for 30 minutes.

Spread ice cream over the cookie crust.

Sprinkle with nuts and freeze again for about an hour.

Combine butter, powdered sugar, evaporated milk, and chocolate chips in a medium pan.

Bring the fudge mixture to a boil slowly over medium heat, stirring constantly for 8 minutes.

Remove from heat and let fudge cool.

Pour fudge, when cool over ice cream layer. *(Sprinkle with more nuts if desired.)*

Return the dessert to the freezer. Serve frozen.

SERVING TEENS AND KIDS

Cheese-Rice Cereal Appetizers

{Makes 60 servings}

1 cup butter, softened

2 cups flour

2 cups grated cheddar cheese *(sharp is best)*

2 cups of crisped rice cereal

Combine butter, grated cheese, and flour in a large bowl.

Add cereal and stir well.

Form the mixture into golf-ball size and place about 2 inches apart on an ungreased cookie sheet.

Flatten the balls slightly with a fork.

Bake 10 minutes at 375 degrees.

Serve warm or store in an airtight container.

Cheddar Biscuit Balls

{Makes about 18}

2½ cups of dry biscuit mix
1 lb. spicy or Italian ground sausage, cooked
4 cups grated cheddar cheese

Mix all ingredients in a medium bowl.
Roll into golf ball size balls.
Place on a greased cookie sheet.
Bake at 350 degrees for 10–12 minutes.
Serve hot.

Note:
These make a great brunch appetizer and can be made up ahead
of time and refrigerated or frozen until ready to bake.
Thaw before baking.

Personal Pizza Appetizers

{Makes 20 small pizzas}

1 lb. sliced pepperoni or cooked Italian sausage
2 cups grated mozzarella cheese
1 (26-oz.) can pizza sauce
2 pkgs. refrigerated biscuits or sandwich thins *(20 total)*
½ cup grated Parmesan cheese
mushrooms *(optional)*
olives *(optional)*
peppers *(optional)*

Roll and stretch biscuit dough, on a floured surface into 20 4-inch circles, then place on a greased baking sheet.

Spread 2 tablespoons of pizza sauce on each dough circle.

Sprinkle grated cheese on top.

Top each circle with your choice of meat or combination of toppings.

Bake at 425 degrees for about 10 minutes.

Serve while warm.

BLT Dip

{Makes 2¾ cups}

1 cup sour cream
¾ cup mayonnaise
½ cup real bacon bits, or crumbled cooked bacon
½ cup chopped sundried tomatoes
salt
dash pepper

Mix ingredients and chill.

Serve with crackers or pita chips

Note:
For a nice presentation, line a bowl with a large lettuce leaf
and fill with dip.

Can't Resist 'Em Hot Wings

{Makes 30–35}

1½ cup flour
1 tsp. paprika
¾ tsp. cayenne pepper
¾ tsp. salt
30–35 chicken wings

¾ cup butter
¾ cup hot sauce
pinch of black pepper
¼ tsp. minced garlic *(or less if you like less garlic)*
vegetable oil

Combine flour, paprika, cayenne pepper, and salt. Put mixture in a zippered plastic bag.

Place 5 or 6 wings at a time in bag and shake to coat. Put coated chicken into one or two glass baking dishes.

Cover chicken with plastic wrap and refrigerate for 1 hour.

Meanwhile, in a small saucepan over medium-low heat, combine butter, hot sauce, pepper, and garlic in a small saucepan and heat. Remove from heat.

Heat about 1½ inches of vegetable oil to 350–375 degrees in a frying pan with deep sides. (Use a thermometer to keep heat constant between 350 and 375 degrees.)

Fry coated wings in hot oil for 10–15 minutes until chicken is cooked and crispy.

Remove wings from oil. (If you are making these ahead of time, refrigerate. When ready to serve, put them on a pan in a 350-degree oven to reheat.)

Pour sauce over wings when ready to serve and put extra sauce in a bowl for dipping.

Serve these with lemonade to help cut the spiciness of the hot wings.

Chinese Chicken Kabob Appetizers

{Makes 8–10}

¾ cup soy sauce
¼ cup sugar or sugar substitute
1 Tbsp. olive oil
¼ tsp. minced garlic
½ tsp. ground ginger *(fresh is fabulous)*
2 large chicken breasts, skinned and boned

8 green onions, chopped
½ lb. small, fresh mushrooms
1 green or red pepper, cubed
wooden skewers *(soaked in water overnight, if possible)*

Combine soy sauce, sugar, oil, garlic, and ginger in a medium bowl,

Cut the chicken into bite-size cubes.

Add chicken and onions to the bowl.

Let meat marinate at least 30 minutes. If you're going to let it marinate overnight, don't add the onions until 30 minutes before building the kabobs.

Alternate ingredients onto the skewers, including the mushrooms and peppers.

Place on a broiler rack or on a cooling rack set inside another pan.

Broil about 5 inches away from the flame. Baste occasionally with sauce, turn once after about 3 minutes, and cook another 3 minutes until done.

Serve hot.

Baked French Toast Casserole

{Makes 12 servings}

1 loaf thick-sliced or regular bread
1 (8-oz.) pkg. cream cheese
10 eggs
2 cups milk

3 Tbsp. butter, melted
1 tsp. cinnamon
⅓ cup maple syrup (or 1 cup blueberries)

Cut crusts off bread and cube into 1-inch pieces.

Place in a greased 9x13 baking dish.

Mix cream cheese with a few eggs at a time, then slowly add milk, butter, and cinnamon.

Pour this mixture over the bread, and between layers if layers are used.

Cover and refrigerate overnight.

Preheat oven to 350 degrees and bake for 35–40 minutes.

Serve with maple syrup or blueberry topping (below).

Blueberry topping: Mix 1 cup sugar with 2 tablespoons cornstarch. Add 1 cup water. Over medium heat, bring mixture to a boil and boil for 2–3 minutes. Add 1 cup blueberries and return to boil. Reduce heat to low and simmer for 8–10 minutes. Stir in 1 Tbsp. butter. Serve warm over casserole.

Note:
Make this recipe ahead and refrigerate overnight
until ready to serve.

Fantastical Banana Pops

{Makes 12}

6 large bananas
½ cup honey
1 (16-oz.) pkg. chocolate chips, melted *(use double-boiler or microwave)*
½ cup each nuts, crisped rice cereal, cornflakes, or coconut
12 wooden craft sticks

Peel bananas and cut in half through the middle.

Insert a wooden craft stick into the banana.

Cover bananas in honey or melted chocolate.

Immediately roll bananas in nuts, crisped rice cereal, corn flakes, or coconut.

Eat right away or wrap in plastic and freeze for a frozen banana later.

For directions on how to melt chocolate, see **page 75**.

Cake Mix Cookies

{Makes 3 dozen}

1 box cake mix, any flavor
⅓ cup vegetable oil
2 eggs
chopped nuts *(optional)*
frosting, if desired

Preheat oven to 375 degrees.

Combine cake mix, oil, eggs, and nuts (if desired) in a large bowl.

Stir until thoroughly moistened.

Shape dough into 1-inch balls and place 2 inches apart on ungreased cookie sheets.

Flatten to ¼-inch thickness, using the bottom of a glass dipped in flour.

Bake for 6–8 minutes. Cool for one minute and remove to wire rack.

Frost, if desired, when cookies are slightly warm for a glazed frosting.

Decorate with sprinkles or powdered sugar. Some frosting can be purchased with free candy sprinkles included.

Cocoa Ice Cream Snowballs

{Makes 16}

2 cups chocolate-flavored crisped rice cereal
1 cup coconut
1 cup chopped peanuts
½ gallon ice cream, any flavor

Combine cereal, coconut, and nuts in a mixing bowl.

Scoop large scoops of ice cream and roll in mixture.

Put in freezer to set, and then serve on a cone or in a dish.

Cookie Pizza

{Makes 8–10 servings}

1 egg
½ cup brown sugar
¼ cup sugar
½ cup butter, softened
1 tsp. vanilla extract
1¼ cups flour
½ tsp. baking soda

Preheat oven to 350 degrees.

Grease a pizza pan with shortening.

Combine egg, sugars, butter, and vanilla in a bowl and mix with a wooden spoon.

Add flour and baking soda to mixture and stir into a stiff dough.

Spread dough to edge of pizza pan.

Bake 15 minutes, or until golden brown.

Let cool, decorate, and cut into wedges with a pizza cutter.

Decoration Possibilities:

* chocolate cookie crumbs, peanut butter, chocolate chips, tiny marshmallows
* chocolate frosting, grated white chocolate *(for "cheese")*, colored candies
* raspberry or strawberry jam, grated white chocolate *(for "cheese")*, fruit roll-up *(for "pepperoni")*

Cookie Pops

{Makes 48}

1 box yellow cake mix
1 cup flour
8 Tbsp. butter, melted
¼ cup honey
2 large eggs
1 cup colored sugar sprinkles
48 wooden craft sticks

Preheat oven to 375 degrees.

Combine cake mix, flour, melted butter, honey, and eggs in a large mixing bowl.

Mix on low for 2 minutes, scraping sides of bowl as you mix, to make a stiff dough.

Flour hands lightly and shape dough into 1-inch balls.

Roll each ball in sprinkles and place on a greased cookie sheet 2 inches apart.

Bake 8–12 minutes, or until edges are light brown.

Remove from oven and immediately insert a stick halfway into each cookie.

Let cool another 1–2 minutes and remove to wire rack to cool completely.

Store by wrapping in clear or colored plastic wrap.

Homemade Pretzels

{Makes 16}

1½ cups flour
½ cup grated cheese
2 lbs. butter, softened
1 tsp. baking powder
⅔ cup milk
1 egg
coarse salt *(optional)*

Spray cookie sheet with cooking spray.

Mix all ingredients, except egg and salt, with a wooden spoon.

Sprinkle cutting board with flour.

Cut dough into 2 balls, roll dough in flour, and knead 10 times.

Divide each ball into 8 pieces, and roll each piece into a 12-inch rope.

Shape and twist dough into pretzel shapes and place on cookie sheet.

Beat egg and brush onto pretzels.

Sprinkle with coarse salt, if desired.

Bake 15–20 minutes until golden brown. Place on wire rack to cool.

Top or serve with nacho cheese, mustard, or peanut butter.

Kitten-Cat Bars

{Makes 12–15 bars}

2 sleeves rectangular saltines
1¼ cup brown sugar
½ cup butter
½ cup milk
1 cup peanut butter, divided
1 cup semisweet chocolate chips *(12 oz.)*

Remove ¼ crackers from one sleeve and crush finely. Set aside.

Place one layer of crackers in a 9x13 dish.

Combine cracker crumbs, brown sugar, butter, and milk in a large saucepan, and bring to a boil over medium heat.

Boil for 5 minutes, stirring constantly.

Remove from heat and stir in ½ cup of peanut butter until melted.

Pour mixture over crackers in pan.

Top with another layer of crackers.

Combine chocolate chips with remaining ½ cup peanut butter in a medium glass bowl. Microwave for 2 minutes on medium power. Remove and stir until smooth.

Pour mixture over bars and spread carefully to cover crackers.

Cool and cut into bars.

Crisped Rice Cereal Squares

{Makes 24 servings}

3 Tbsp. butter

1 (10-oz.) pkg. miniature marshmallows

6 cups crisped rice cereal *(or any cereal)*

Melt the butter and marshmallows together in a large pan over medium heat.

Stir cereal into marshmallow mixture.

Form into a pan or other shape while mixture is still warm, and let cool.

Fun Variations:

- Try chocolate crisped cereal or fruity flavored cereal.
- *Crispy Cups*: Form cups with mixture in muffin tins and serve with ice cream or pudding.
- *Pinewood Derby Cars*: Cut mixture into rectangles to use as the body of a car. Use frosting to adhere cookies as wheels. Use colored candies for headlights and taillights. Use half of a chocolate sandwich cookie for a steering wheel.
- *Christmas Wreaths*: Add green food coloring and shape into wreaths. Add cinnamon candies for holly berries.
- *Snowmen*: Stack three different-sized balls while still warm and decorate with candy and frosting.
- *Footballs*: Form mixture into football shapes, frost with chocolate frosting, and pipe "laces" with white frosting.
- *Faces*: Cut cooled mixture into circles with a glass or cookie cutter sprayed with cooking spray and decorate with candies and frosting to look like faces.
- *Balloon shapes*: cut cooled mixture into circles with a glass or cookie cutter sprayed with cooking spray, decorate with bright-colored frosting and candies, and use licorice strings for balloon strings.

Marshmallow Popcorn Balls

{Makes 8–10}

3 Tbsp. butter
1 (10-oz.) pkg. mini marshmallows
8 cups of air-popped popcorn

Pop popcorn and remove any unpopped kernels.

Melt butter and marshmallows together in a large pan over medium heat.

Stir popcorn into marshmallow mixture.

Butter hands and form into balls while popcorn is still warm.

Place on a cookie sheet to cool.

Store in separate plastic sandwich bags or wrap in plastic wrap.

Variation: Chocolate Popcorn Balls

Use 4 Tbsp. butter
Add ¼ cup light brown sugar to marshmallow mixture.
Add 8 oz. semisweet chocolate chips and melt together.

Purple Cow Drink

{Makes 5 six-ounce servings}

1 (6-oz.) can frozen grape juice concentrate
1 cup milk
2 cups vanilla ice cream
5 purple grapes

Mix juice and milk in a blender.

Add ice cream and blend again.

Serve with straws that have been pushed through purple grapes.

Quick Breakfast Egg Casserole

{Makes one 9x13 pan, or 12 servings}

1 (8-oz.) can refrigerated crescent rolls

8 oz. thin sandwich ham *(or 8 bacon strips cooked, chopped)*

6 eggs

½ cup milk

½ tsp. pepper

1 cup cheddar cheese, grated

1 cup mozzarella cheese, grated

Preheat oven to 350 degrees.

Spray 9x13 pan with cooking spray.

Line bottom of pan with crescent rolls and press to seal seams, making a solid crust.

Sprinkle ham or bacon on crust.

Beat eggs, add milk and pepper, and pour over the ham.

Top with both cheeses.

Bake for 25 minutes.

Note:
Some like a dollop of sour cream on top when served
for a European flare.

Surprise-Inside Chocolate Peanut Butter Balls

{Makes 5 dozen}

¼ cup butter
1½ cups peanut butter
4 cups confectioners' sugar
2 tsp. vanilla extract
2 cups semisweet chocolate chips
candies and nuts *(optional)*

Cream together butter, peanut butter, confectioners' sugar, and vanilla extract. Knead if necessary.

Melt chocolate chips over low heat.

Shape dough into 1-inch balls.

Insert a peanut, chocolate chip, candy-coated milk chocolate piece, or peanut butter-flavored candy for a surprise inside. If you use a variety of these things, the person eating it will never know what they are going to get in the middle of theirs!

Dip into melted chocolate chips. Place them on a cookie sheet lined with wax paper.

Refrigerate for 15–30 minutes or overnight. Store in airtight container.

Surprisingly Wonderful Cookie Candy Bars

{Makes 70}

1 (16-oz.) box buttery round crackers
peanut butter
semisweet or dark chocolate chips

Spread peanut butter on half of the crackers.

Top with remaining crackers.

Melt chocolate using a double boiler or in a microwave.

Dip each cracker sandwich, covering completely.

Place on wire rack and let set.

Zippered Bag Homemade Ice Cream

{Makes about 3 cups}

¾ cup whole milk
1 cup whipping cream
⅓ cup sugar
½ tsp vanilla extract

1 quart-size zippered plastic bag
1 gallon-size zippered plastic bag
ice
rock salt

Place all ingredients into quart-size bag and seal tightly.

Put quart-size bag inside gallon-size bag.

Pack gallon-size bag with ice and sprinkle ice with rock salt. Seal well.

Wrap double-bagged mixture with several layers of newspaper. Wrap again with duct tape.

Shake or toss from one person to another for 15–20 minutes.

Open and eat!

Variation: You can place the first bag into a large can and pack with ice and rock salt. Seal, wrap with newspaper, and tape. This method allows children to roll the can back and forth to thicken the ice cream.

SCOUTS AND CAMPING

CAMPING FOOD IDEAS

It is possible to go camping or backpacking and still enjoy a nice meal. Creativity and planning can result in a pleasant eating experience with good nutrition and little cleanup. Camping can also mean more to the campers if they have prepared their own food or menu. Listed below are some of the most successful ideas from many camping experiences. Some are relative "no-brainers" in preparation; others will take a little effort before or during the outing.

Foil dinners are always a favorite and fun meal.

Some suggestions:

carrots, chicken breast, ground beef, onions, thickly sliced potato slices, 1 tsp. dry gravy mix *(makes a nice sauce as the dinner cooks)*

- If the dinners will be not be refrigerated for any length of time, freeze the entire dinner, and it will thaw as you go.
- Even if you don't like onions, placing them on both sides of the main meal will help other ingredients to not stick to the foil.
- Don't forget some seasoning! A teaspoon of powdered gravy mix is perfect to add.
- Make sure to double-wrap the dinners and make the seams on opposite sides for security.

Meatloaf can be made ahead of time, wrapped around a strong stick, wrapped in foil and cooked over an open fire.

Canned chili or chowder can be eaten in a bread bowl—no dishes to clean up.

Tuna in a pouch is lighter weight and easier to open than the canned version.

Pancakes can be cooked, frozen, and then reheated on a skillet—no messy batter cleanup.

One pan chili-spaghetti: boil spaghetti noodles in a pan, then add a can of chili, grated cheese, and onions on top.

Cup of soup: no clean up (Make sure to pack and take trash out of the campsite.)

Boil-in-bag Rice leaves little mess. Supplement with MREs (Meals Ready to Eat)

Instant potatoes or cartons of dehydrated hash browns (Don't forget the water source.)

Freeze-dried eggs, add bacon bits or precooked bacon for flavor.

Boxed noodle dinners with a can of chicken or tuna makes a great hot meal.

Orange-flavored powdered drinks and powdered lemonade are easier than soda to carry.

Orange-flavored powdered drinks and packages of apple cider mix taste great when served hot!

Instant hot chocolate, of course, but add in some mini marshmallows as a surprise

Canned biscuits can be cooked on a stick for a hot bread.

"Just add water" cheese biscuit mixes add extra flavor.

Canned stew

Instant oatmeal

Corn on the cob needs no refrigeration and can be cooked in its husk in the coals.

Popcorn in a foil pan for popping over the fire.

Snacks: dried fruit, nuts, granola, popcorn, dry salami slices, popcorn in a foil pan, beef jerky (try making it at home!)

Transport eggs in plastic storage containers already unshelled, add a few drops of water to keep them moist. Freeze if you like.

Freeze bottles of water to keep food cool in transit, then use the water to drink or cook with.

Campers can plan and share meals and share the load to be carried.

Dutch Oven Sweet Pineapple Cake—Easy as Pie!

{Makes 12}

1 (20-oz.) can pineapple slices
1 box yellow or white cake mix
4 Tbsp. butter or margarine

Line a 10- or 12-inch Dutch oven with foil.

Pour sliced pineapple and juice in bottom of pan.

Sprinkle cake mix on top of pineapple.

Stir juice and cake mix slightly.

Cut squares of butter or margarine on top.

Bake 45 minutes with coals on top and bottom. Check regularly to control heat.

Gobs of Camping Granola

{Makes 28 half-cup servings}

Dry ingredients
1½ cups raw almonds, whole or chopped
10 cups uncooked rolled oats
1 cup sunflower seeds
1 cup peanuts
1 cup dried fruit (apples, apricots, raisins)

Wet ingredients
½ cup vegetable oil
½ cup honey
¾ cup orange juice concentrate

Preheat oven to 300 degrees.

Mix dry ingredients in a large bowl.

Pour wet ingredients into a saucepan. Heat and stir until combined.

Let cool until cool to the touch.

Pour wet ingredients over the dry ingredients and mix well with hands.

Spread mixture onto 2 large cookie sheets.

Bake slowly for 1¼ hours.

Remove from oven, stirring as mixture cools.

Turn off oven, place granola back in oven, and let dry overnight.

Place granola in bags or airtight containers when dry.

Dutch Oven Pizza

{Makes 1 pizza, or about 8 servings}

1 lb. loaf frozen bread dough, thawed (or use ready-made 12-inch pizza crust)
1 (8-oz.) container pizza sauce
3 cups grated mozzarella cheese
pepperoni slices
cooking spray

Preheat a 12-inch Dutch oven by placing it on top of nine hot charcoal briquettes. Put the lid on top and place twenty briquettes on lid.

Use ready-made pizza crust or stretch bread dough to 12-inch circle.

Spread sauce onto dough, sprinkle cheese over sauce, and top with pepperoni.

Spray some oil into the Dutch oven to keep pizza from sticking.

Place the pizza in oven and replace lid.

Keep oven out of cold, windy areas, as this can affect its temperature.

Bake for approximately 10 minutes if you use ready-made crust, and approximately 12–15 minutes for frozen bread dough.

> *Note:*
> You can buy ready-made pizza crusts, but you can also make
> your own crusts ahead of time and precook them, which
> will speed up cooking time significantly.

Heavenly Dutch Oven Peach Cobbler

{Makes 12 one-cup servings}

Fruit
½ (#10) can peaches with syrup
1 cup frozen blackberries *(optional)*

Dry ingredients
3 cups flour
1 cup oatmeal
2½ cups brown sugar
1½ Tbsp. baking powder
1–1½ Tbsp. cinnamon
pinch of salt

Put fruit into a large Dutch oven.

Mix all dry ingredients together and pour over the fruit.

Cut a stick of butter and place on top of dry mixture.

Put on the lid.

Place sixteen briquettes on bottom of pan and twelve on top.

Cook for 23 minutes.

Note:
This can be baked in an oven. If so, remove Dutch oven lid for
the last 5 minutes to crisp top of cobbler.

Ooey-Gooey Chocolate Pocket S'mores

{Yield variable}

large marshmallows
chocolate chips

Cut slits into a marshmallow.

Repeat with a second marshmallow.

Place a chocolate chip inside slits.

Place both marshmallows on a roasting stick, making sure the slit sides face each other in the middle.

Roast over a campfire and enjoy!

"Love in a Tortilla" S'moritos

{Makes 10}

10 flour tortillas
peanut butter
marshmallow crème
mini marshmallows
chocolate chips
bananas
apple bits
coconut flakes

Spread peanut butter or marshmallow crème on flour tortillas.

Top with any or all other ingredients.

Fold like a burrito and wrap in aluminum foil.

Place in coals or on a barbecue grill, and let everything melt slowly.

Open carefully and eat.

REFRESHMENTS

Variety Mini Cheesecakes

{Makes 18}

1 (12-oz.) pkg. vanilla wafer cookies
2 (8-oz.) pkgs. cream cheese
¾ cup sugar
2 eggs
1 tsp. vanilla or lemon juice
18 regular-size muffin papers

Toppings: cherry or apple pie filling, fresh fruits (slice of strawberry or mandarin orange), dust with cocoa powder, swirl with a heated chocolate dessert glaze, or nuts

Preheat oven to 350 degrees.

Place muffin papers into muffin pans, and place a vanilla wafer cookie in each paper.

Beat cream cheese, sugar, eggs, and vanilla in a medium bowl until fluffy.

Fill each muffin paper two-thirds full with cream cheese mixture.

Bake 15 minutes.

Let cool before decorating.

Store in refrigerator.

Note:
For more variety, use your favorite cheesecake recipe: chocolate, pumpkin, lemon, and so on.

Unique (but Simple) Refreshments

Sometimes it isn't the cost or the time involved in refreshments, but a slight tweak on an old standard that can make things fun but easy for the preparer.

Here is a list of possibilities:

Brownies

- brownies decorated simply, but giving a selection to choose from.
- brownies with an assortment of flavored frostings
- brownies topped with a variety of toppings: nuts, coconut, sprinkles, colorful candies, drizzled caramel, powdered sugar, chocolate chips *(The assortment will look like a box of chocolates.)*
- brownie sundaes offered with more than one flavor of ice cream.

Unique Ice Cream Floats

- Try vanilla ice cream, orange sherbet, or lime sherbet with a variety of sodas, like orange, grape, strawberry, grapefruit, and root beer. No need to always have root beer. No additional cost is incurred using this creative twist and allows guests to choose their own combinations.(*Note: Filling the glass first with cold soda and then adding the ice cream will create much less foaming.)*

Cookie Bar

- Providing a variety of cookies with a variety of frostings and candies will allow guests to create their own original cookie.

Hot Chocolate

- Hot chocolate with whipped cream and a peppermint stick to stir with
- Hot apple cider or wassail with whipped cream and caramel syrup swirl

Ice Cream Sandwiches

- Provide a variety of homemade cookies, allow guests to choose two cookies, and put a scoop of ice cream between them to create a unique ice cream sandwich. If you can have several choices of ice cream, half the fun will be choosing from the many possibilities. The edges can also be rolled in candy sprinkles for even more fun.

Cheesecake Assortment

- This is an elegant way to give guests a choice without a lot of extra effort. Purchase plain cheesecakes, but serve them with a variety of toppings: cherry pie filling, chocolate sauce drizzle, lemon pie filling, raspberry sauce, strawberry jam, blueberry pie filling, sprinkled cocoa powder, caramel ice cream topping, chopped nuts or just a twist of lime and a lime slice. More than the adventure of choosing one of these is the beautiful sight it makes on a table or tray to see the choices

Strawberry Croissants

- Make a mixture of fresh strawberries and whipped topping. Slice croissants and fill them with strawberry mixture. Drizzle with chocolate syrup. *(Before filling, slice croissants in half, dip the entire top in melted chocolate chips and let cool.)*

Pound Cake Creations

- Pound cake is one of the easiest ways to use your imagination to create a dessert. Different sherbets, ice cream flavors, or whipped topping and fruit can create any flavor of dessert, but it looks like a lot of work went into it.

Chocolate Raspberry Dream Cake

- By using any chocolate layer cake, you can create an elegant dessert like those served in restaurants. There is something rich in adding a few fresh or frozen raspberries and a simple raspberry sauce to a plate of chocolate cake.

POTLUCK EVENTS

A potluck is a great way to get groups together and share in the food preparation. But without a little planning or organization, a potluck can be less than you had hoped for.

Try some of these tried-and-true options for a successful event.

THE POTLUCK:
SUCCESSFUL, YET SIMPLE TO ORGANIZE!

Set the date and make a list of your guests and determine how many will possibly come.

Plan a basic menu or theme.

Some suggestions:

Appetizers only	Chili	Italian	Mexican
Oriental	Salads	Casserole	Soups

Make-Your-Own Banana Split

Make-Your-Own Pizza

Barbecue *(or just bring your own meat to grill)*

"Before and After" *(Serve hors d'oeuvres and have guests bring baby pics)*

Once you have a theme, make sure that everyone has an assignment. You can let them choose, but they must let you know what they want to bring, so you don't have too many other guests bringing the same thing. You will need main dishes, breads, desserts, and beverages, and you will most likely provide the dishes, napkins and decorations.

One way to do this—if it is a neighborhood party or large group—is to assign the even-numbered homes a main dish and odd-numbered homes a dessert. Then you, or your organizing group, can provide the rest. By doing this, you won't need to spend much time talking to people or keeping track of what they are bringing.

When making assignments, try to assign guests who aren't sure whether they are coming things that won't be missed or that you can easily replace yourself, such as napkins, extra salad, or water to drink.

INDEX

Appetizers

Side Dishes

Main Courses

Desserts

Camping

About the Author

Sydney Lee Shardlow Cline grew up in Southern California. She is a graduate of Brigham Young University, the former owner of Upper Crust Catering, and a retired elementary school teacher. Sydney and her husband, Bruce, have six sons and one daughter and thirteen grandchildren. This has given her plenty of opportunities to feed large crowds from her own kitchen!

Through many years of family cooking, catering, and serving in multiple capacities in her church, Sydney began to record the things she learned about organizing and preparing food. It was especially during her six years as a stake Young Women president that many food-related needs arose.

HOW TO SCORE

by Antony Lishak

CONTENTS

THE BIG QUESTIONS ...

Have you ever asked yourself what it
is that makes a great goal-scorer great?

**Why don't their
shots always fly
over the bar?**

**Why don't they
panic and suddenly
freeze at the sight
of an open goal?**

And, most importantly ...

HOW CAN YOU BECOME LIKE THAT?

AND THE EVEN BIGGER ANSWERS .

REMEMBER This book
will not turn you into a
sure-shot sharp-shooting
superstar. But it will help
you sharpen your striker
skills. Read the book,
practise a lot and you can
improve your chances of
scoring the winning goal!

The most important thing you need to know

To get a ball to go where you want it to, you have to kick it in exactly the right spot. This is called the **sweet spot**. It's just below the middle of the ball.

As long as your ball isn't too big or too heavy then, with practise, you should be able to find the sweet spot. The trick is being able to find it every time!

BASIC BALL CONTROL

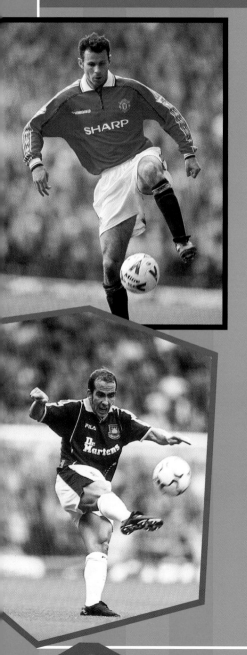

Ball control is about **balance** and **body position.** While you're kicking a ball with one foot, your whole body weight is balancing on the other foot (the **standing foot**). To kick the ball well, you must be very good at standing on one leg.

Most people are either right-footed or left-footed. If you are equally happy kicking with either foot then **you're one of the lucky ones!** If you are not, try this exercise:

How to make your weak foot stronger

Practise this exercise using only your weaker foot for half an hour a day.

1. Stand about five metres away from a wall and kick a ball against it.

2. Kick it gently at first, but as you become more confident, move further away from the wall and kick the ball harder.

3. Make sure you are making a good contact with the ball. Try to become as good at finding the sweet spot with your weaker foot as you are with your other foot.

Play keepy-uppy

Playing keepy-uppy is a great way to learn how to control a ball. Most professional footballers have spent their childhoods doing it! Remember to stay balanced, and keep your weight over the ball.

KICKING A DEAD BALL

It is important to be able to kick a ball straight. This skill is as important in passing as it is in shooting. **The shortest distance between any two points is a straight line.** So if you want to pass the ball to another player as quickly as possible or fire in a shot before the goalie can dive to cover it – learn to kick the ball in a straight line.

The goalie saw this one coming!

Goal!

How to kick a dead ball straight

Place the ball. Draw a long **straight** chalk line on the ground. Practise kicking a ball along the line. As you get better, make the line longer and kick the ball harder. Practise with both feet. Learn from your mistakes. For example, if the ball keeps veering off to the right, change your body position to correct it and think about where on the ball your foot is making contact.

COACHING TIPS

Think about hitting the sweet spot every time. Remember to lean your body weight over the ball. Leaning back makes the ball go high.

CONTROLLING A MOVING BALL

When a ball is moving, you have less time to get into position and less time to think about what you want to do with it. To get the ball under control **before** you shoot, get the ball just in front of your kicking foot. This is the place

easy zone

where you can have comfortable control of the ball. This place is called the **easy zone**. Once you've got the ball where you want it, you can treat it like a dead ball.

How to control a moving ball 1

Put a plastic hoop on the ground in front of you. Get a friend to throw a ball at you and try to **cushion** it so that it stops inside the hoop. The area inside the hoop represents the easy zone. Remember to use both feet to control the ball.

How to control a moving ball 2

Here is an activity you can do by yourself. You'll need a ball and a wall. Practise kicking the ball against the wall. When the ball comes back to you, cushion it with your standing foot so that it stops in your easy zone. When it's under control, kick the ball towards the wall again.

As you become more confident move further away from the wall and try to control the ball faster.

 COACHING TIP

Remember your body shape. Make sure you get behind the ball when it comes to you so that you don't have to stretch. Stretching for a ball ruins your body shape and affects your balance. And keep your eye on the ball!

KICKING A MOVING BALL

This skill is all about watching the ball carefully, getting into position quickly, deciding what you want to do with the ball when it comes to you, and making sure you get the best contact you can with it.

How to kick a moving ball

You will need a ball and between three and six people. Mark out an area about ten metres square with chalk. The idea is to keep a ball inside this area and to keep it moving. Each person is allowed to touch the ball only once, so there is no chance for them to control it first. The passer has to make sure the pass is accurate, and the receiver has to get into a comfortable position to receive the ball. Count how many passes you can manage before the ball goes out of control.

 **COACHING TIP**

Be careful not to kick the ball too hard. Kicking a ball that's already moving increases its speed.

BENDING THE BALL

To **bend** a ball, you must kick the sweet spot, but instead of kicking straight through it (to make the ball go straight) you have to come at it from a slight angle, to make the ball spin. This is an *advanced kicking skill!*

 COACHING TIP

Don't vary the angle a lot. If you do, it's very easy to **slice** it out of control.

How to bend the ball

You will need:
- a goal (you can use jumpers to mark the goal)
- as many balls as you can get, so you don't have to keep running off to get the ball back
- some sort of barrier, like a row of dustbins

What you have to do

1 Stand about twenty metres away from the goal.

2 Put the dustbins or other barrier half way between you and the goal.

3 Put the balls in a line in front of you.

4 Decide which side of the barrier you want to bend the ball round.

5 Shoot at the goal!

Goal

Barrier

COACHING TIP

Stay balanced, lean your body weight over the ball and try to make a good connection with the sweet spot. You'll probably slice the ball at first, but don't be put off – keep trying!

CHIPPING THE BALL

The **chip** is a kicking skill used to surprise those goalies who rush off their line. It can also be used to clear defensive walls on free kicks. It's cheeky, it's effective and it looks good. But it looks far easier than it is.

How to chip the ball

Practise kicking the ball so it rises quickly in front of you. For this kicking skill do **not** kick the sweet spot. Stab your foot sharply under the ball and don't follow through after contact. Think about connecting with the centre of your foot, not your toes. Like bending the ball, this is an **advanced skill** that marks out the great goal-scorers from the rest!

 COACHING TIP

No matter how good you get at chipping a ball, don't use it too often in a game. An important part of making this shot really effective is the element of surprise!

HEADING THE BALL

Whether you have to leap up to reach a ball, stoop down or even dive to make contact, there are two things you've got to get right ...

- **Keep your eyes open and watch the ball.**
- **Hit the sweet spot with your forehead.**

The power behind a header comes from your neck muscles. The more you practise, the stronger your muscles become and the harder your headers will be to stop!

Play header-tennis

Play header-tennis with a friend. This trains you to keep your eye on the ball and encourages you to use your neck muscles to direct the ball forward. Gradually move further apart as you get more confident!

COACHING TIP

To begin with you'll want to close your eyes as the ball gets near your head, but don't! Remember, make contact with your forehead. Any higher and you won't see the ball. Any lower and you'll hurt your nose!

TAKING PENALTIES

Cup-ties are often settled on a **penalty** shoot-out. The most important part of a penalty kick is **not** the point of contact. It is those few seconds **before** the kick, when the striker has to decide what to do with the ball.

There are two main ways of trying to get the ball past the goalie – you can either **blast** the ball or you can **place** the ball. Both ways work, so decide which way is most comfortable for you. Once you have made up your mind, stick with it!

Taking a penalty requires lots of concentration.

18

Practise taking penalties

You'll need a friend, a ball and a goal (preferably painted on a wall so that you don't have to keep chasing after the ball). Take turns at being the penalty taker and the goalie. Try out all the possible variations – blast or place, will it be high or low, right, left or middle? See what works for you.

GETTING THE BALL PAST THE GOALIE

In a real game, you aren't going to get many shots at an empty net. So practise with a goalie as much as you can.

When you play with a goalie, you have to decide whether to blast or pass, chip or swerve. You might have to decide whether to shoot, or whether to pass to another player. And you must decide very quickly. Practise is the only way to get good at this.

Heading the ball is another way to surprise the goalie!

How to keep the goalie working hard

You will need:

- five footballs
- a goal
- a goalie

Try to score with each ball. Watch what the goalie is doing. Choose any of the methods we have looked at in this book. You are allowed only one shot per ball. See how many goals you can score.

WHEN THE GOALIE GETS IN THE WAY

Sometimes a goalie will move towards you to stop you scoring. Sometimes a defender will try to move you away from the **goalmouth**.

This ball got through!

This cuts down the area of the goal you can shoot straight into. When this happens, you have to decide if it is worth trying to shoot ...

Sometimes it is safer to pass to another player.

... or whether you should pass to a player who is in a better position.

How to get past the goalie

You will need:
- ⬣ five footballs ⬡ a goal ⬣ a goalie

Try to score with each ball, using any of the methods in this book. Start your attack on goal from the **wing** and get the goalie to come out towards you. You have only one shot per ball. See how many goals you can score.

🏃 **COACHING TIP**

Make sure that you attack from both wings so that you can practise shooting with both your right and your left foot.

HEALTHY LIVING

It doesn't matter how hard or how far you can kick a ball if you're not fit. Top athletes are super-fit. They keep their bodies in good condition by eating the right things and by taking lots of exercise. They try not to harm their bodies by smoking or drinking alcohol.

Healthy hint 1 – Food

Food is a footballer's energy source. Eating the right foods, and not eating too much, will help you stay fit.

Avoid greasy foods – make sure you eat lots of fresh fruit and vegetables.

*Build up the **carbohydrates** –* they give you energy.

Don't overeat – especially just before exercise.

Healthy hint 2 – Drink

You sweat to cool down when you're hot. Make sure you replace that lost liquid after, and if possible, while you exercise.

Still drinks are best – fizzy drinks can unsettle your stomach if you are exercising. Water is best of all.

Don't gulp your drink – sip it slowly. Drinking too fast will also unsettle your stomach.

Don't overdo it – drinking little and often is better than drinking lots in one go!

Healthy hint 3 – Warming up and warming down

You need to warm up your body before you do any exercise. If you don't, you can hurt your muscles. Stretch the muscles on your legs, arms, back, stomach and neck gently to warm them up. When you have finished exercising, do some more gentle stretching. This helps your muscles to recover more quickly. It is called warming down.

Healthy hint 4 – Stamina not strength

As a young footballer, you should try to build up your **stamina** rather than your muscles. This means building up how long you can exercise for. Jogging is a good way of building up your stamina. But don't overdo it. Look after your body. It's the only one you have!

GOAL CELEBRATIONS

So you've worked on your skills, you've got yourself fit and you've been picked as striker for your team. You shoot and score the winning goal with just two minutes left to play. **Well done!**

But there's one more thing you've got to learn. No goal is complete unless it has been celebrated! So here is a selection of famous goal celebrations that you might want to use ... and there are many more!

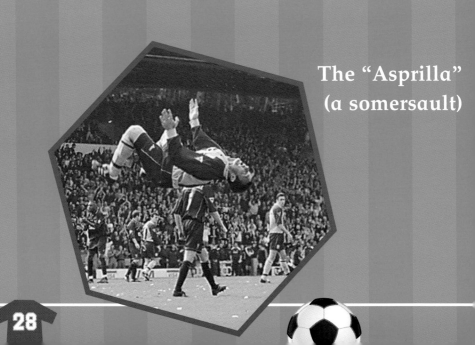

The "Asprilla"
(a somersault)

The simple
nching-the-air

The "Here's-my-belly"
(lifting your shirt over
your head)

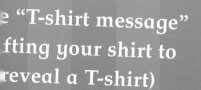

e "T-shirt message"
fting your shirt to
reveal a T-shirt)

The "Beckham"
or "Wrighty"
(a statue-like pose)

The "Roger Milla"
(dancing round the
corner flag)

The "Klinsmann"
(a full length dive)

UNSCIENTIFIC METHODS!

Throughout this book we have looked at ways to improve your footballing skills. But many players have other ways to improve their game.

wearing lucky charms

always putting the left boot on first

kissing the head of your goalie

not putting your shirt on until just before you step on to the pitch

wearing lucky pants

There is no scientific reason why any of these should work, but hundreds of footballers use them. They may help get the players' minds focused on the game and settle their nerves before the whistle.

Whatever method you choose,

GOOD LUCK!

GLOSSARY

bend: making the ball swerve in the air

blast: hitting the ball really hard

carbohydrate: the energy content in food

chip: making ball rise very quickly, usually to go over a
defensive wall or a goalie

cushion: using your body to take the pace out of a moving
ball and make it easier to control

easy zone: the area in front of a player where the ball can
be most easily controlled

goalmouth: the area of a pitch that is directly in front
of the goal

penalty: an unchallenged shot taken from a spot 12
yards away from the goal

place: trying to put the ball in a specific part of the goal

slice: miss hitting the ball, making it veer off in the
wrong direction

stamina: the energy to keep going

standing foot: the non-kicking foot

sweet spot: the ideal part of the ball to connect with

wing: the area of the pitch closest to the touch lines

INDEX